GiveGet

GiveGet

photographs by

Jason Bell

edited by Guy Harrington

dewi lewis media

Cancer Research UK would like to thank Jason Bell, and Guy Harrington at Soho Management and everyone at TK Maxx, for having the vision and resolve to support this project.

TK Maxx and Jason Bell are donating all profits and royalties from the sale of this book to Cancer Research UK.*

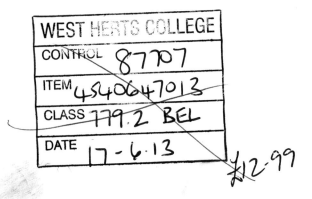
* see publisher's page at the end of the book for details

GiveGet is an amazing campaign for Cancer Research UK. We have a chain of more than 600 charity shops that rely on generous donations from the public for their success. GiveGet is one of the biggest charity collections ever undertaken in the UK and we hope it will raise more than half a million pounds towards our life-saving research.

We are incredibly grateful to Jason Bell and Soho Management for encouraging such an impressive collection of celebrities to support GiveGet and for creating such inspiring photographs. The end result is this beautiful book, which we hope you will enjoy. Our thanks go to Jason and to every celebrity who has so kindly donated their time, and in some cases their clothing, to support Cancer Research UK.

And finally, we would like to thank TK Maxx, the retailer, who has underwritten all the costs of the campaign and helped us to organise the nationwide efforts. Without their support, GiveGet could never have happened and we hope that this provides inspiration to other big companies in the future.

:Professor Alex Markham
Chief Executive
Cancer Research UK

Charity Number: 1089464

First and foremost a huge thank you yet again to Guy Harrington, for pulling it out of the bag as usual, and in an ever-decreasing amount of time. Thanks to Joel Bygraves at Soho Media, for providing inspiration, and to all at Soho Management, especially to my agent, Fiona Rooke-Ley, and to Nikki Carter. I also could not have done it without the following: my gorgeous assistant, Lindsey Hopkinson; Sven Langmanis; Gayle Rinkoff and Celine, Austique Boutique, Ashley Isham, Philip Treacy, Proportion Mannequins, and Rootstein Display Mannequins, who generously supported her; Mel Arter; Sophie Chevalier; Deborah Dolce, an extraordinary woman who understands that the way to get someone to give their best is to leave them to get on with it, and TK Maxx, for making the whole project possible; Jo Murphy, for her calmness and unparalleled project-management skills; Freud Communications, especially Paul Melody (my nbgf), Rebecca Hirst, Max Dundas, Jack Freud, Shilpa Patel and Claire Salvetti; Metro Soho Studios; James English Studios; Vim Jethwa, the night watchman at the Retouch Hutch; and of course my favourite inscrutable publisher Dewi Lewis (who has never said whether or not he likes my work but after three books together I am beginning to suspect he might).

Everyone knows someone who has had cancer. My brother has had it. Twice. My best friend's mother had it. His mother-in-law had it. My stepfather's wife had it. Some have survived and some have not. This book is about changing that ratio.

Everyone with cancer wants to hear two words: "All clear". Their families want to hear those words. Cancer Research UK is about more people hearing those words. And how amazing that the simple act of giving your old clothes to a Cancer Research UK shop can make that happen.

So GiveGet is about giving clothes so that Cancer Research UK gets.

Some of the pictures in this book are lighthearted. I worried about this. Perhaps it is in poor taste to laugh about cancer. But to refuse to laugh about it is to assert that cancer is always fatal. Yet more and more people do hear the words "All clear." Cancer is no longer a death sentence. My brother has survived it. Twice.

Jason Bell

Elijah Wood
Actor

Johnny Vegas
Comedian, Actor

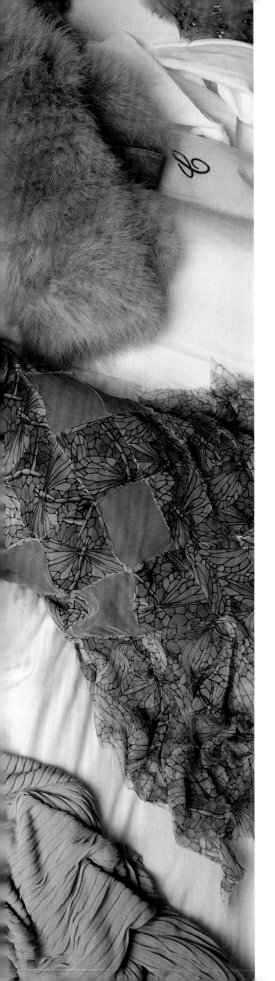

Jamelia
Musician

Cynthia Nixon
Actor

Raza Jaffrey
Actor

Preeya Kalidas
Actor

Kate Winslet
Actor

Kirsty Young
Newsreader

Krishnan Guru-Murthy
Newsreader

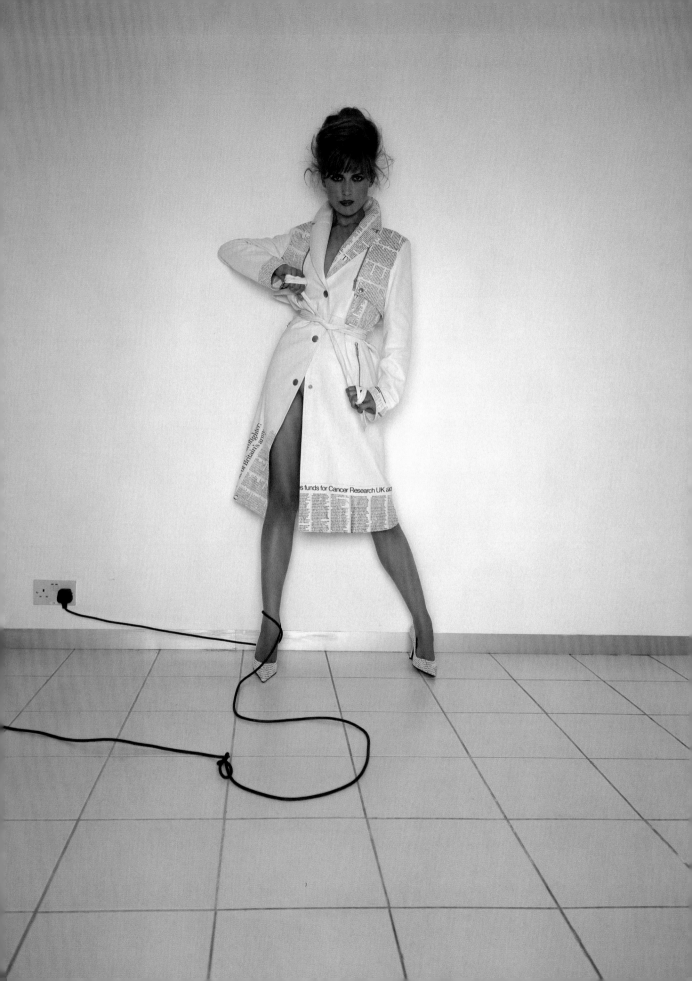

Katie Derham
Newsreader

Minnie Driver
Actor, Musician

Charlie Hunnam
Actor

Charlotte Church
Musician

Lisa Butcher
Model

Jamie Theakston
Actor, Presenter

Bryn Terfel
Bass-Baritone

Luke Perry
Actor

Nell McAndrew
Model, Presenter

Mackenzie Crook
Actor

Leah Wood
Musician

Mis-Teeq
Musicians

Max Beesley
Actor

Katie Melua
Musician

Driscal
Musicians

Lisa B
Model

Tamara Rojo
Prima Ballerina

Liam Neeson
Actor

This book is being sold through TK Maxx stores and independent book retailers. TK Maxx, Jason Bell and Dewi Lewis Media will make individual contributions to Cancer Research UK as follows:

Jason Bell will donate all proceeds from the sale of the book. *

TK Maxx will donate all proceeds from the sale of the book, less its costs. Costs will be covered once 2,715 books are sold by TK Maxx. This represents 45.2% of the 6,000 books to be offered for sale by TK Maxx. *

Dewi Lewis Media Ltd, the publisher of the book, will donate £1.50 per book sold through independent book stores. *

* These contributions will be paid to Cancer Research UK Trading Limited which gives its taxable profits to Cancer Research UK.

First published in the UK in 2004 by

Dewi Lewis Media Ltd
8 Broomfield Road, Heaton Moor
Stockport SK4 4ND, England

www.dewilewismedia.com
www.dewillewispublishing.com
www.jasonbellphoto.com

Photographs © Jason Bell
This Edition © Dewi Lewis Media Ltd

ISBN: 0-9546843-1-1

Editor: Guy Harrington
Photo Retouching: Vim at Soho Retouch
Design & Artwork Production: Dewi Lewis, DLP Digital Studio
Print: EBS, Verona

With thanks to Epson UK